A Civilization Project Book

ESKIMOS

BY SUSAN PURDY
AND CASS R. SANDAK

Illustrations by James Watling
Diagrams by Jane F. Kendall

Franklin Watts   New York/London/Toronto/Sydney   1982

Contents

Library of Congress Cataloging in Publication Data

Purdy, Susan Gold
  Eskimos.

  (A civilization project book)
  Includes index.
  Summary: Instructions for duplicating such Eskimo
artifacts as charms, kayaks, masks, games, soap carv-
ings, and dolls.
  1. Eskimos—Juvenile literature. 2. Eskimo craft—
Juvenile literature. [1. Eskimo craft. 2. Eskimos. 3.
Handicraft] I. Sandak, Cass R.
II. Title. III. Series.
E99.E7P87   745.5'08997   82-7007
ISBN 0-531-04456-4   AACR2

Life in the Arctic

Eskimos are the native inhabitants of the arctic and subarctic regions of North America. They are widely scattered but have a very uniform culture ingeniously suited to survival in the Arctic. At present, there are about 70,000 Eskimos: 30,000 in Greenland, 22,000 in Alaska, and 16,000 in Canada. In addition, about 1,100 Eskimos live in the Chukchi Peninsula of northeastern Siberia.

Eskimos inhabit a belt of land that extends roughly 600 miles (972 km) on each side of the Arctic Circle. Mostly they live along the icy ocean shores. Villages are seldom more than a hundred people. These are scattered westward from Greenland, across Labrador, northern Canada, throughout the frontier west of Hudson Bay, and along the Alaskan and Siberian coasts.

Most anthropologists believe the Eskimos originated in Siberia and crossed to Alaska as long ago as four thousand years ago. Their shared language, physical type, and culture point to origins in Asia along with other Indian tribes.

In the winter, temperatures in the Arctic region regularly plummet to 60°F (16°C) below zero. In the summer it seldom gets as warm as 60°F (16°C). For two months in the winter, the land is in almost total darkness as the sun remains below the horizon. Near the Arctic Circle, the sun shines day and night during the few short weeks of summer.

Eskimos live by fishing and game hunting. During the warm-

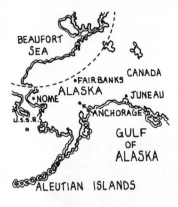

ALASKA

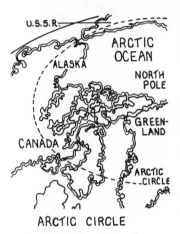

ARCTIC CIRCLE

er months, Eskimo families set up caribou skin tents. In winter, many Eskimos even camp over frozen areas of sea where fishing and hunting are best. Eskimo hunters travel on sleds. These used to be made from pieces of bone and driftwood, but now metal runners and even snowmobiles are used. The traditional Eskimo sleds are drawn by teams of strong dogs called huskies.

Eskimos call themselves *Inuit*. The word means "the people." The name Eskimo was given to them by the Algonquin Indians. The word means "people who eat their food raw." Vitamins and minerals are plentiful in the uncooked fish and meat that form the basis of the Eskimo diet. Whale and seal blubber are delicacies. A few berries and tender plant shoots might be eaten in summertime, but agriculture is not usually practiced.

The animals of the Arctic region are very important to the Eskimo way of life. Eskimos hunt whales, seals, and walruses with harpoons. The bow and arrow, nets and hooks for fish, and nets on long poles for capturing birds are sometimes used. Animal products provide food, clothing, heat, and even shelter. Fibers from bird feathers are spun into thread. Seal meat is eaten and seal sinews are made into thread. Sinew swells when it is wet and helps to keep clothing waterproof. Oil from various animals is burned in lamps. Fur is made into clothing and fur scraps are fashioned into toys and dolls. Tough walrus hide is made into harnesses for dogsled teams. The ivory tusks are turned into buckles, needles, and ornaments. Many Eskimos are skilled artists in carving bone, ivory, and antler.

Modern Eskimos buy much of their clothing. But traditionally they have used the skins of caribou and seals to make their hooded jackets, or *parkas*. These are often trimmed with pieces of fox skin. Boots, called *mukluks*, are made from sealskin with bottoms of walrus hide. Mittens keep their hands warm. Women wear cotton dresses called *kuspuks* over their fur parkas.

Today, most Eskimos are Christians. Their former religion stressed a belief in spirits and acts of mercy—caring for the sick, blind, aged, and helpless. Eskimos welcome orphans into their homes and families. They share almost everything they have. Only clothing, tools, charms, toys, and dogs are regarded as personal property. Until recently, crime was almost unknown among Eskimos.

Eskimos love to visit with each other. They have adopted the European custom of shaking hands, although they used to greet each other by rubbing noses. In Alaska, they celebrate the killing of a whale with dancing and feasting. Flat drums, made from hoops of bone or wood covered with deerskin, are popular musical instruments. They have archery and boxing contests, and play ball games and blanket toss.

All Eskimos are unified by the same basic language—a very complex one. There are two forms of the Eskimo language. *Yupik* is spoken by the Siberian Eskimos and those in the southern part of Alaska. *Inupik* is spoken by Eskimos who live in the northern part of Alaska and in Canada, Labrador, and Greenland. The Eskimos have a strong oral storytelling tradition.

Today books and newspapers are printed in the Eskimo language, and most young Eskimos study in schools. Although the modern world intrudes, the Eskimos still have a vital and active culture. Many Eskimos have turned away from hunting and fishing and now work on fishing boats, in mines, in canneries, and on docks. But others practice a way of life developed hundreds of years ago. They are a close-knit hunting society. Theirs is a hard yet fun-loving way of life and they are proud to be Eskimos.

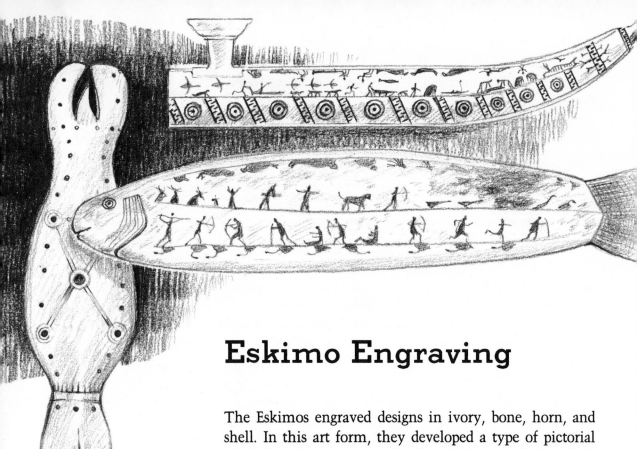

Eskimo Engraving

The Eskimos engraved designs in ivory, bone, horn, and shell. In this art form, they developed a type of pictorial symbol similar to pictographs that told stories of their daily lives and hunting exploits. Sometimes, too, they used purely ornamental geometric designs. They decorated many objects, including tobacco pipe stems usually made from long thin bones or walrus ivory, whale bone clubs, elkhorn spoons, ivory hat and button decorations, and their medicine men's amulets and other instruments and tools.

Engravings were made with a graver's tool. This is an instrument that consists of a wooden handle, with a notched end for a finger rest, and a quartz point or iron pin inserted in the tip. The incised lines of the bone or other material were filled in with red ocher or black soot. Then the piece was wiped clean, so that only the colored lines remained against the white background.

Materials you will need:
Clean, dry pieces of bone with all sinew removed (ask your butcher to save the bones and cut them for you), sharply pointed long nail or awl or other sharp engraving tool, piece of charcoal or cork, safety matches, paper towels, pencil, scrap paper

1. Boil bones for one hour and then remove the marrow. Clean, wash, and dry them completely.

2. Plan your design on paper with a pencil, following the basic contours of the bone, as in Figure 1. Notice where it is long, or thin, or wide, or curved, etc. Try to tell a simple adventure story using stick figures (for example, boy, girl, house, boat, fish under waves of water, carrying fish). Or, write your name and draw a geometric design. Straight lines are easier to make than curves.

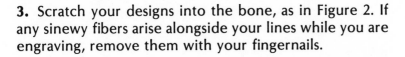

Figure 1

3. Scratch your designs into the bone, as in Figure 2. If any sinewy fibers arise alongside your lines while you are engraving, remove them with your fingernails.

4. Rub charcoal or soot from burned cork into the scratch lines. Rub across the surface of the bone, as in Figure 3. This will force the color into the grooves of the lines.

5. Use a paper towel to wipe across the bone to remove the excess, leaving only the color in the lines.

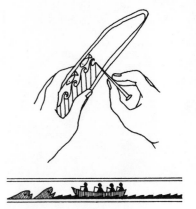

Figure 2

Figure 3

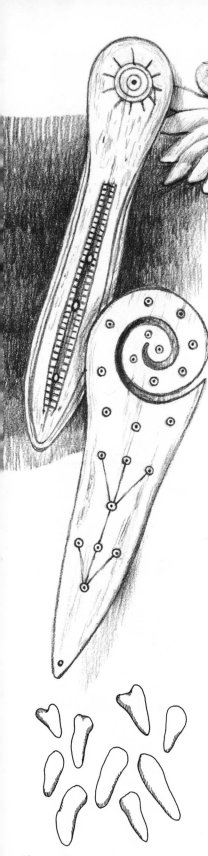

Eskimo Ornaments

Eskimo men and women adorned themselves with charms and jewelry—necklaces, lip plugs, and ornamental buttons that showed animals. These buttons were not used to fasten pieces of clothing but were decorative. Objects of this type were made from animal products—bones, antlers, teeth, tusks, fur, or sinew. They were simple in design and usually showed animal or geometric motifs.

Eskimo artifacts like these are used both for decoration and as magical amulets to bring good luck while hunting and fishing. The Eskimo tooth necklace was thought to give the hunter strength and power over sea mammals—seals, whales, and walruses—as he went to hunt them. The Eskimo hat ornament is usually made from ivory or bone and is tied with a piece of sinew to the hunter's hat.

SEA MAMMAL TOOTH NECKLACE

Materials you will need:
Self-hardening clay, nail, sandpaper, string or heavy cord about 15 inches (37.5 cm) long

1. Model animal "tooth" shapes from self-hardening clay. The shapes should be irregular and uneven, as shown in Figure 1. You will need about forty shapes that are approximately ½ inch (1.25 cm) wide.

Figure 1

8

2. Use a nail to make a hole for stringing the teeth for your necklace before the clay hardens (see Figure 2). Be sure the holes are large enough to thread the string or cord through them.

3. Allow the clay to harden. Sand any rough edges.

4. String the teeth on the cord. When you have strung enough teeth to make a necklace, tie the cord together.

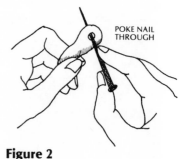

POKE NAIL
THROUGH

Figure 2

IVORY HUNTING HAT ORNAMENT

Materials you will need:
Tongue depressor, Exacto knife, sandpaper, felt-tip marking pens, nail

1. Use the Exacto knife and sandpaper to shape the tongue depressor into the form shown in Figure 1.

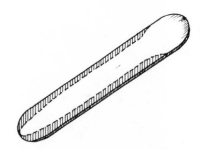

Figure 1

2. Draw an eye and sun disk design at the upper and wider end of the form you have made (see Figure 2).

3. Decorate the length of the stick with the design motif shown in Figure 3.

4. Make a nail hole in the top of the ornament. This is for tying the ornament to a hunting hat.

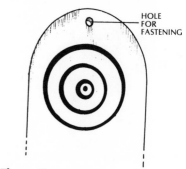

HOLE
FOR
FASTENING

Figure 2

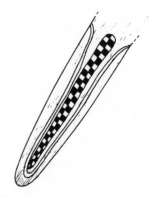

Figure 3

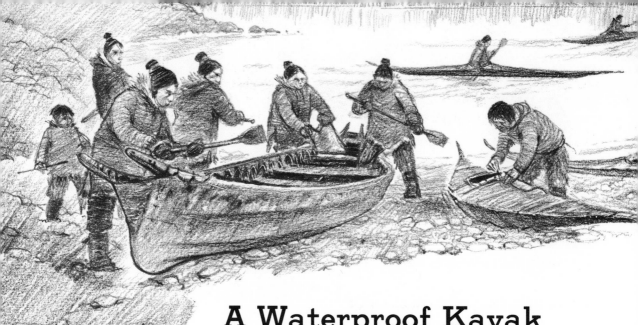

A Waterproof Kayak

There are two forms of Eskimo boats, both made from frames covered with skin. The open-topped boat is called the *umiak*. It sometimes has a sail, but is usually propelled by a paddle. The *kayak* is a much smaller skin boat built on a wooden framework, covered with sealskin. It usually has a single hole in the top in which a single paddler sits. A 19-foot (5-m) kayak weighs only about 32 pounds (14.5 kg). The kayak is used for hunting. Archaeological evidence shows that kayaks were used as long as two thousand years ago.

The kayak consists of a basic framework of small strips of wood running lengthwise and brought together at the bow and stern. They are connected by curved cross-bracing ribs fastened with rawhide cords. Resting on top of the crosspieces which support the top of the boat is a circular opening surrounded by whalebone or a wooden hoop. The surface is covered with sealskin. The skins have been tanned and the hair has been removed. They are sewn together with sinew cord. Seams are oiled or coated with reindeer tallow to make them waterproof, and the surface of the kayak is oiled and dried thoroughly before putting it in the water. The paddler wears a waterproof parka made from seal intestines sewn together, with an attached hood. When the hem of the waterproof parka is tied around the outside of the manhole rim, the paddler is totally waterproof. Skilled paddlers can turn over and stay dry.

Kayak sizes and styles vary by region, as do paddles. Kayaks use both single- and double-bladed paddles. Single-bladed paddles are more common, but double-bladed ones give more speed. Paddles or oars were often painted red, black, and white, in patterns that showed ownership.

The Eskimos sometimes painted magic pictures on the outside of the kayak. They believed that human faces painted on the undersides would keep the kayak from tipping over. Often a crocodilelike mythological animal was painted on the sides of the umiaks. Other times, paintings on the boats showed sea lions and ducks caught in a net, or whales.

Materials you will need:
Flexible, strong wire such as electrical wire or coat hanger, wire cutters, plastic-coated cloth tape 1½ inches (4 cm) wide, scissors, tape measure or ruler, thin spool or thread wire, wooden tongue depressor or ice cream stick, jackknife (optional), felt-tip markers

1. Use the wire cutters to cut one strip of heavy wire or coat hanger 20 inches (50 cm) long and another strip 11 inches (28 cm) long.

2. Bend the 20-inch (50-cm) strip in half (Figure 1) so that each leg is 10 inches (25 cm) long. The wires should bow out in the center and taper at each end.

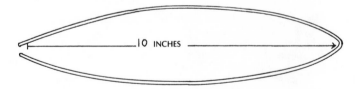

10 INCHES

Figure 1

3. Fit the 11-inch (28-cm) length down the center of the two legs. Wrap about 1 inch (2.5 cm) of its end around the center bend. Tape the join to hold it in place, as in Figure 2.

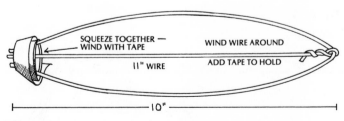

SQUEEZE TOGETHER — WIND WITH TAPE   WIND WIRE AROUND

11" WIRE   ADD TAPE TO HOLD

10"

Figure 2

4. Make a seat hole by cutting a 6-inch (15-cm) piece of heavy wire and bending it into a hoop with a 2-inch (5-cm) diameter (Figure 3). Overlap the ends slightly and tape them to hold.

5. Use spool or thread wire to form a cross bracing on the underside of the kayak. Wrap wire around and between each of the three legs. Repeat this at several intervals. This makes the kayak strong and lets it hold its shape (Figure 4).

6. Fasten the seat hoop between the two side legs of the kayak with spool wire. The hole should be positioned slightly back from the center, as shown in Figure 5: 6¼ inches (16 cm) from the front end.

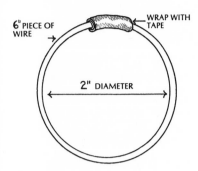

6" PIECE OF WIRE

WRAP WITH TAPE

2" DIAMETER

Figure 3

7. Put tape over the wires holding the hoop to the sides. Add spool wire to make a cross brace on the top of the kayak between the side legs just in front and just in back of the seat hoop (Figure 5).

8. Make a "skin" for the kayak out of cloth tape. Cut a strip of tape 1½ inches (4 cm) wide and 11 inches (28 cm) long. Put the tape sticky side up on a table and lay the kayak on its side along the tape (Figure 6).

9. Cut off the end angles of the tape to conform to the shape of the kayak.

10. Press the edges of the tape over onto the wire frame. Smooth the edges.

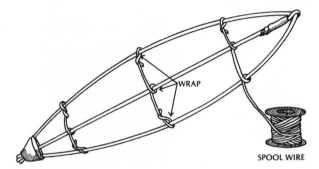

WRAP

SPOOL WIRE

Figure 4

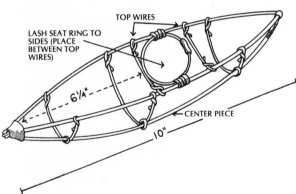

TOP WIRES

LASH SEAT RING TO SIDES (PLACE BETWEEN TOP WIRES)

6¼"

CENTER PIECE

10"

Figure 5

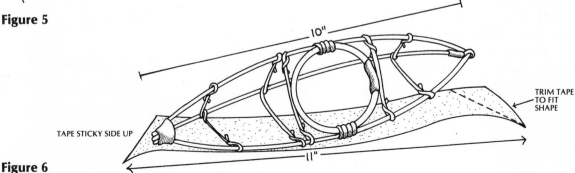

10"

TRIM TAPE TO FIT SHAPE

TAPE STICKY SIDE UP

11"

Figure 6

11. Repeat this taping procedure on the other side of the kayak (Figure 7). The side tape should overlap slightly along the bottom center rib. Be sure that all tapes overlap slightly and that there are no holes where the framework shows through. If the kayak is taped properly, it will be waterproof and will float.

Figure 7

12. Cover the top of the kayak frame with tapered pieces of tape cut as shown (see Figure 8). Press the edges of the tape flat and smooth them down over the sides of the kayak. Cut center sections to fit around the seat hoop as shown.

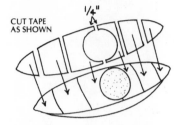

Figure 8

13. To cover the seat hoop, cut a 6-inch (15-cm) length of tape. Fold down one third of the width onto itself. Press the sticky sides together, leaving one third of the sticky surface exposed (Figure 9). Wrap this piece of tape into a ring with the *sticky side out* (Figure 10).

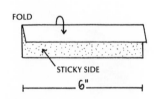

Figure 9

14. Set the tape ring down into the seat hoop with the sticky edge of the tape facing down and against the wire hoop. Press the tape against the wire hoop. The folded tape edge should stick up, making a raised lip (Figure 11).

15. Whittle a paddle from a wooden tongue depressor or ice cream stick. Use permanent ink felt markers to decorate the kayak and paddles with designs (see Figure 12).

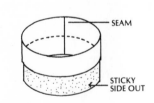

Figure 10

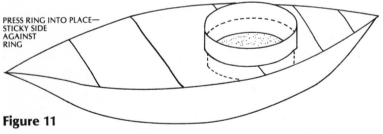

Figure 11

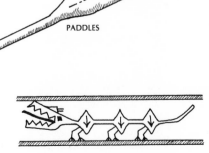

Figure 12

UMIAK ALLIGATOR
CALLED "PAL-RAI-UK" ⟶

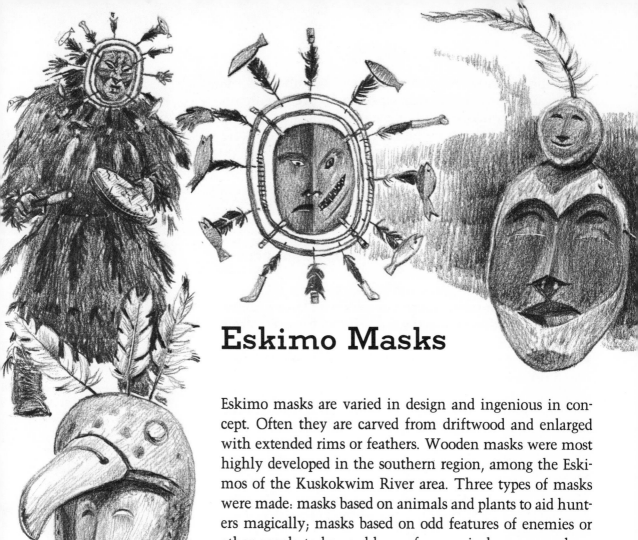

Eskimo Masks

Eskimo masks are varied in design and ingenious in concept. Often they are carved from driftwood and enlarged with extended rims or feathers. Wooden masks were most highly developed in the southern region, among the Eskimos of the Kuskokwim River area. Three types of masks were made: masks based on animals and plants to aid hunters magically; masks based on odd features of enemies or other people to be used by performers in humorous plays; and masks made for the shaman, or medicine man.

Masks with human faces were given an animal-like character to symbolize an animal "soul." The Eskimos believed that animals have souls. Thus, masks sometimes had half human and half animal faces. The Eskimos believed that the animals they killed would be reincarnated and restored to life. They thought that the animals should not be afraid to meet the hunter. The animal should know it would be treated fairly.

Ritual dancing masks used by the Eskimos were designed to influence the being which "lived" in the mask. This soul was immortal, and was honored by the dance. If the mask represented an animal, the dance and the mask were to propitiate the creature and bring about plenty of game. Animal's souls were thus invited to the feast, to enjoy the song and dance, and accept the honors. Thus, the appeasement of the animals was a prime object of the masks. They were not designed purely for the sake of art. Popular motifs for masks, as well as for other Eskimo art forms, were animals like the seal, walrus, fish, whale, reindeer, otter, fox, wolf, and bear. The Eskimo masks were usually painted white or blue with red highlights.

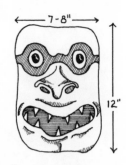

Figure 1

Materials you will need:
Salt dough (see box), colored feathers, bits and scraps of wooden sticks (optional), modeling tools or toothpicks, plastic knife, sandpaper, glue, tempera paints, paper, pencil

1. Use paper and pencil to plan your mask. Select a specific motif—a character designed to make you laugh, the face of an owl, bird, fish or whale, or a half-man, half-animal face, such as the one shown in Figure 1. The mask should be about 12 inches (30.5 cm) long and 7 inches (18 cm) or 8 inches (20.5 cm) wide.

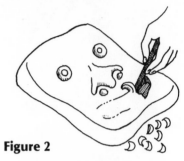

Figure 2

2. Prepare the clay, then build up the basic form.

3. Use tools to model the features. Be bold and simple. Avoid small details, as in Figure 2.

4. Poke toothpick holes in the rim so you can later glue on feathers.

Figure 3

5. Let the clay dry thoroughly.

6. Sand the rough edges.

7. Paint your mask.

8. Decorate the outer edge of the mask by sticking in or gluing feathers and bits of wood shaped like wings, paws, tails, or teeth. (See Figure 3.)

SALT DOUGH RECIPE

1 cup salt
2 cups all-purpose flour
1 cup water
2-3 drops vegetable oil

Mix the ingredients together and roll out. Shape the dough. Sun-dry the pieces or bake them at 200°F (93°C) for about two hours for ¼-inch (.6-cm) thick pieces, longer for thicker pieces. Or bake at 200°F. (93°C) overnight with door of oven ajar. Do not use higher temperature or pieces will turn brown and crack. The purpose of baking is to dehydrate the dough, *not* to bake it. Dried pieces may be sanded before painting.

Eskimo Games

Eskimo children and adults play many games. Children's toys are fashioned out of materials readily available: bone or ivory, animal skin and fur, and sometimes wood. Ball games are popular. The ball is generally filled with moss and covered with sealskin and decorated with fringed strips of hide.

ROTATING BALLS ("ESKIMO YO-YO")

One popular Eskimo ball game uses two small leather balls on strings, attached to a handle, or tied together with a knot. The object is to rotate the two balls in *opposite* directions at the same time. This is also sometimes known as Eskimo yo-yo.

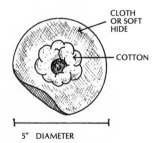

CLOTH OR SOFT HIDE

COTTON

5" DIAMETER

Figure 1

Materials you will need:
Cotton fabric or soft animal hide, scissors, needle and thread, string, two small pebbles or two pennies or bottle caps, cotton batting or poly fiberfill

1. Make two circles of cotton fabric or soft animal hide, each 5 inches (12.5 cm) in diameter, as in Figure 1.

2. Cover two pebbles or pennies with cotton and wrap them separately in each 5-inch (12.5-cm) circle of cloth or skin (Figure 1).

3. Overlap the edges of the circle and stitch them down, to make a ball shape, as in Figure 2. The ball does not have to be perfectly round to work.

4. Cut two lengths of string, one 26 inches (66 cm), the other 30 inches (76 cm).

5. Use about 10 inches (25 cm) of each piece to tie around a cloth ball as if you were wrapping a gift with ribbon (Figure 3). The string crosses the ball in two directions. It is then knotted to itself. The rest of the length hangs loose.

6. In a few places, sew the string onto the ball's cloth covering using an overwrap stitch (Figure 4). This will secure the string so it does not slide off when the balls are swinging.

7. Hold the loose string ends and knot them together (Figure 5). One string with a ball should be about 14 inches (35.5 cm), the other about 18 inches (45.5 cm). Be sure that one string is longer than the other, even if the dimensions are not exact.

To play (Figure 6):
Hold the knotted end of the string in your hand, and move it so that the balls rotate in opposite directions. This is easier said than done! There is a secret to it. Begin by holding the short string aside and rotating the ball with the long one alone first. When it is moving well, send the second ball in the opposite direction, all the while keeping your hand moving *up and down*. Never rotate your hand or the balls will rotate in the *same* direction.

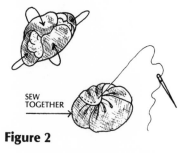

SEW TOGETHER

Figure 2

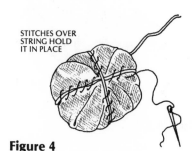

FINISHED BALL

APPROX. 1 3/4" DIAMETER

Figure 3

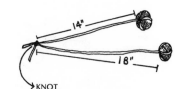

STITCHES OVER STRING HOLD IT IN PLACE

Figure 4

14"

18"

KNOT

Figure 5

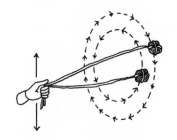

Figure 6

17

AJEGAUNG (HOLES-AND-PIN GAME)

Another game of skill is called *ajegaung*. This is the holes-and-pin game, played by tossing an object with holes in it into the air and catching it by one of its holes on a pin. This is the Eskimo version of the medieval court jester's cup and ball on a string. The object caught used by the Eskimo is often the dried bleached skull or pelvis bone of a small animal, with a pin made of bone. Sometimes small ivory animal carvings are used.

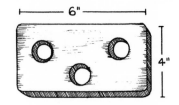

Figure 1

Materials you will need:
Piece of rectangular or curved medium weight wood (e.g., a strip of shingle) or heavy corrugated cardboard or thick plastic, string, an unsharpened pencil, rubber band or tape

1. Prepare a piece of wood, cardboard or plastic with holes. It can be any shape and size, although it should be about the size of your hand or fist. It should be heavy enough to have some weight when tossed into the air. The holes should be large enough for your "pin" to pierce them easily (see Figure 1). An unsharpened pencil makes a good pin.

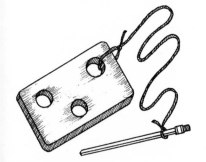

Figure 2

2. Tie one end of a string through a hole in your object, and another end to the "pin." Secure the string on the "pin" by wrapping it with a rubber band or bit of tape (Figure 2).

3. Hold the "pin" in your hand with the point up. Toss the hole-panel into the air. Try to catch it as it falls by piercing one of its holes with the pin (Figure 3).

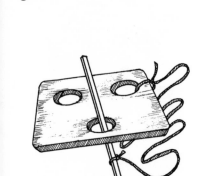

Figure 3

TINGMIUJANG, OR "IMAGES OF BIRDS" (AN ESKIMO DICE GAME)

Gambling is a popular amusement for the Eskimo during the long winter months. One game, *tingmiujang* (meaning "images of birds"), is similar to dice. A set of fifteen small carved figures of birds and/or people is used.

Materials you will need:
Self-hardening clay, toothpick, sandpaper, piece of leather

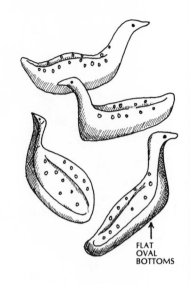

To set up the game:
1. Model small bird shapes approximately 1 inch (2.5 cm) long. Make figures such as those shown or use small figures of men or women. Make as many as will fit in your hand. That is enough to play with, although the Eskimos usually use fifteen pieces. For small hands, model fewer figures.

2. Mark the details with a toothpick.

3. Let the clay harden.

4. Sand the figures smooth.

To play:
1. Players sit around a piece of leather that is used as a game board.

2. The first player shakes the clay figures, then tosses them upward.

3. The figures fall on the leather. Some stand upright, others lie flat or sideways, as in Figure 1.

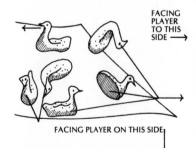

Figure 1

4. Those standing upright belong to whichever player they are facing. This may be the one who tossed, or any other. The standing figures are taken by the player or players they face (see Figure 2).

5. The next player in the circle picks up the remaining pieces and tosses them. The player who faces the pieces wins them.

6. Throw by turns until the last figure has been taken.

7. The player who has the greatest number of figures wins the game.

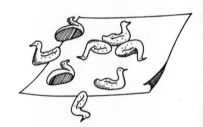

FACING PLAYER TO THIS SIDE →

FACING PLAYER ON THIS SIDE

Figure 2

An Ice Scoop

The Eskimos use many tools for fishing and hunting. These range from harpoons and hooks to special ice scoops. Ice scoops are used to dip out the loose ice that forms in fishing holes or seal holes. The round frame is traditionally made from a bent bone, laced with whalebone, with a long sturdy handle attached. Miniature ice scoops are made for children to play with and to help clear away ice.

Materials you will need:
Flexible tree branch about ¼ inch (.5 cm) to ½ inch (1 cm) in diameter, a heavier stick about 24 inches (61 cm) long up to ½ inch (1 cm) or 1 inch (2.5 cm) in diameter, whittling knife, scissors, spool wire, button thread or string

1. Make the net frame by bending the flexible branch into a hoop with a circumference of about 16 inches (40.5 cm). The diameter will be roughly 5 inches to 6 inches (12.5 cm to 15 cm). Lash the overlapping ends together to hold.

2. Use a knife to notch an even number of narrow spots all around the rim (Figure 1) to hold the netting knots.

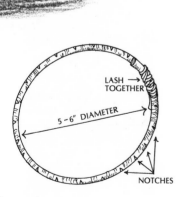

LASH TOGETHER

5 - 6" DIAMETER

NOTCHES

Figure 1

3. Tie wire or string tightly across the hoop, as shown in Figure 2.

4. Knot the lines in the notches on the opposite side of the frame (Figure 2).

5. Weave the wire across the scoop, knotting it on the opposite side of the frame (Figure 3). It is not critical that the lines be taut, but they should be tied firmly on the rim.

6. Fold a whittled, narrow "tongue" of one stick end over the round circular net frame and back onto itself to form a handle (Figure 4). You can soak the tongue a couple of hours to soften it if necessary. If you cannot make a flexible tongue, split the end of the handle and lash it to the frame as shown (Figure 5).

7. Fasten the tongue to the handle. Add extra lashing to be sure that the handle is firmly attached (Figure 6).

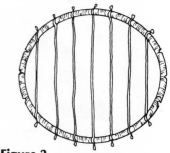

Figure 2

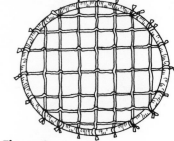

Figure 3

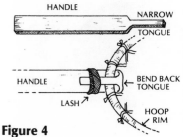

Figure 4

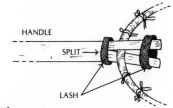

Figure 5

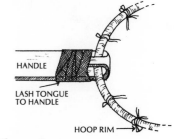

Figure 6

Inside a Snow House

Igloo is the Eskimo word for house. For a long time, most Eskimos have built houses from wood or stone and turf. But the igloo made out of snow blocks is the traditional home that Eskimos used to build as they moved to new hunting places in the cold winter months.

Eskimo hunters still use snow igloos as temporary shelters. An Eskimo can erect a snow house in about an hour or two. He starts by drawing a circle in the snow to mark the place where the igloo will stand. Then he uses a long, swordlike knife to cut blocks out of the snow. In earlier times these snow knives were carved out of animal bone, but modern Eskimos use steel-bladed snow knives.

The snow blocks used in building an igloo are roughly 2 feet (.5 m) long and 1 foot (.3 m) thick and 1 foot (.3 m) high. The blocks are piled in concentric circles in layers, one on top of the other, to build up walls that slope inward to form a dome. A light covering of snow on the outside seals up the cracks between the blocks and acts as insulation.

The entrance to the igloo is a low, narrow tunnel. The

inside of an igloo is one small, circular room. In freezing weather, the inside of the igloo is surprisingly warm. Lamps made from soapstone provide light and warmth, and the temperature rises to nearly 60°F (16°C).

About one-third of the inside of the floor of a snow igloo is taken up by a low "couch" of snow called the *iglerk*. This serves as a bench or table and a bed by night. Caribou hides and sealskins serve as blankets.

The family's food supply, consisting of frozen fish and seals, is stacked in a pile along the wall or just outside the door. Dogs do not come inside the igloo unless they are puppies or pregnant females!

Materials you will need:

Piece of cardboard about 12 inches (30.5 cm) square for the base, one 10-inch (25.5-cm) circular disc of white Styrofoam 1 inch (2.5 cm) thick, glue, compass, pencil, butter knife or scissors end, clay, brown cloth, leather or brown paper bag material, wishbone from chicken or turkey, gray cardboard, thread, toothpicks, sandpaper

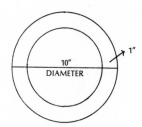

Figure 1

The outer shell:

1. Draw a line across the center of the disc. With a compass, draw a circle 1 inch (2.5 cm) in from the outer edge of the disc (Figure 1).

2. With a butter knife or the end of a scissors, cut this ring from the disc.

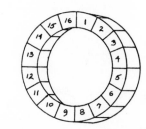

Figure 2

3. With your pencil, divide the ring into sixteen even blocks (Figure 2). (To do this evenly, begin by dividing the ring in quarters. Keep subdividing, and the pieces will be equal in size.)

4. Cut the ring and glue all but one block to the cardboard base as shown in Figure 3. The opening left is where the door will be. You now have the first layer of your igloo.

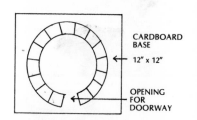

Figure 3

23

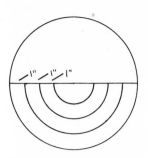

Figure 4

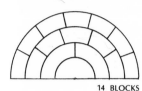

Figure 5

14 BLOCKS

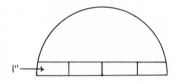

Figure 6

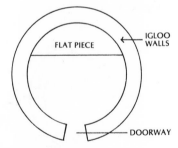

FLAT PIECE

IGLOO WALLS

DOORWAY

Figure 7

BOWLS

Figure 8

5. The disc that is left is now 8 inches (20 cm) across. Draw a line that divides this piece in half. With the compass, draw three circles as shown in Figure 4. The circles should be 1 inch (2.5 cm) apart.

6. Cut the disc in half. Put the unmarked semicircle aside.

7. Cut the marked semicircles into even blocks (Figure 5).

8. With glue, add these blocks to make a second outer layer, still leaving the door opening. Position the blocks so they lean slightly inward. You will use about fourteen blocks.

9. Take the semicircle and cut off a strip 1 inch (2.5 cm) from the flat side (Figure 6). Divide this piece into four blocks.

10. Take what is left of the semicircle and glue it to the inside base of the igloo. The straight edge of this piece should be opposite the entrance. This is the iglerk, or snow couch (Figure 7).

11. Use the four blocks cut from the semicircle to show the entrance tunnel, or porch.

Inside the igloo (see floor plan):
1. Cut caribou skin shapes out of pieces of brown cloth, leather, or brown paper bags. These are used as blankets to cover the iglerk and to keep people warm.

2. Stick two pieces of toothpick about 1½ inches (4 cm) long into the walls near the top of the second layer. This is a rack for drying out clothing and blankets (see floor plan).

3. Out of clay, model a bowl about 1 inch (2.5 cm) across. This represents a lamp in which seal blubber is burned to provide light and warmth.

4. Model a small bowl about ¾ inch (2 cm) across. Eskimos put food in these stone bowls or use them to gather seal blood, which they then drink.

Floor plan of an igloo

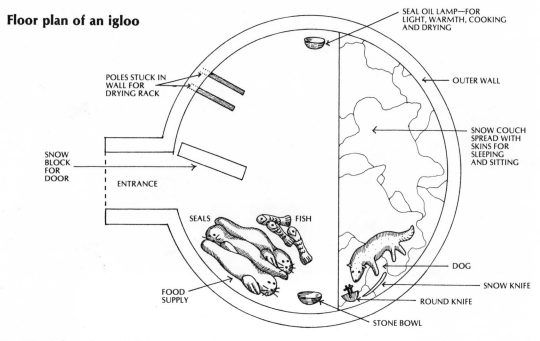

SEAL OIL LAMP—FOR LIGHT, WARMTH, COOKING AND DRYING

POLES STUCK IN WALL FOR DRYING RACK

OUTER WALL

SNOW COUCH SPREAD WITH SKINS FOR SLEEPING AND SITTING

SNOW BLOCK FOR DOOR

ENTRANCE

SEALS

FISH

DOG

SNOW KNIFE

FOOD SUPPLY

ROUND KNIFE

STONE BOWL

5. Model seals and fish out of clay.

a. For fish, start with cylinders of clay about 2 inches (5 cm) long and ½ inch (1.5 cm) wide. Flatten them slightly and model them into fish shapes. Use a toothpick to mark the eyes and scales. Allow the fish to harden.

b. To make seals, start with cylinders of clay about 4 inches (10 cm) long and 1½ inches (4 cm) wide. Model these into seal shapes. Mark the eyes and use broken bits of toothpick to make the seals' whiskers.

6. Make an Eskimo snow knife out of the wishbone of chicken or turkey. Take one side of the wishbone, about 2 inches (5 cm) long, and model it into a swordlike shape by scraping it with a knife and sandpaper.

7. Make a model of an Eskimo round knife used for cutting meat, fish, or animal skins by tying together three bits of toothpick ½ inch (1.5 cm) long, using thread. To make the blade, cut a 1-inch (2.5-cm) circle of gray cardboard. Fold it in half and glue it together. Glue the toothpick construction to the piece of cardboard. This knife, called the *ulu*, is traditionally used only by women.

8. Take two extra blocks and glue them together, so the piece is about 2 inches by 2 inches (5 cm by 5 cm). This is the door. Place it inside the igloo next to the entrance.

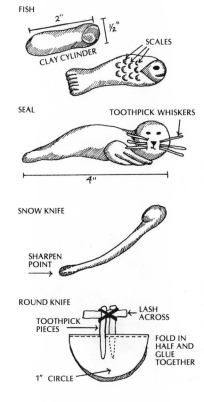

FISH

2"

½"

SCALES

CLAY CYLINDER

SEAL

TOOTHPICK WHISKERS

4"

SNOW KNIFE

SHARPEN POINT

ROUND KNIFE

LASH ACROSS

TOOTHPICK PIECES

FOLD IN HALF AND GLUE TOGETHER

1" CIRCLE

Bear and Whale
Soap Carvings

Carving animals out of soapstone, animal bone, or ivory is still a common artistic activity of Eskimo men. The usual subjects for Eskimo sculpture are the animals they hunt: seals, walruses, fish, whales, reindeer, foxes, wolves, and bears. Eskimo sculpture is realistic in detail, but imaginative and stylized as well. Long ago, figures were often used for magic amulets to bring a good hunt, or were carved for the shaman, who used them in his religious or magic ceremonies. Today, Eskimo sculptures are prized by art collectors around the world.

Materials you will need:
Large cake of soft bath soap, butter knife, pencil, paper. Any size cake of soap will do, but the largest size is easiest to work with

BEAR

Figure 1

1. Decide which animal to carve. Our examples are a bear and a whale, both based on authentic Eskimo carvings. Select an animal hunted by the Eskimos.

2. Draw a sketch of the side view of the animal on the largest side of the soap (Figure 1). On the other sides of the soap, draw the animal as it would look from that side: rear, face and front, right side, left side, and top view (Figure 2).

3. Use the knife to cut out the largest form, revealing the basic shape of the body (Figure 3).

4. Work all around the sides, cutting away a little at a time, to make a three-dimensional figure (Figure 4). The body will have a blocklike look, but it should have rounded edges and a form clearly recognizable from all sides.

5. Use the tip of the knife, a pencil, or a toothpick to engrave the fine details. Make tiny lines to show fur, claws, nostrils, eyes, teeth, fins, etc.

6. You can add color to these lines by drawing over them with a felt-tipped pen.

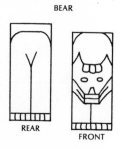

BEAR

REAR

FRONT

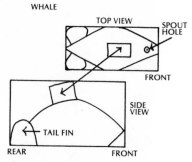

WHALE

TOP VIEW

SPOUT HOLE

FRONT

SIDE VIEW

TAIL FIN

REAR

FRONT

Figure 2

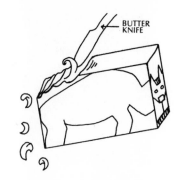

BUTTER KNIFE

Figure 3

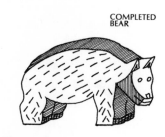

COMPLETED BEAR

Figure 4

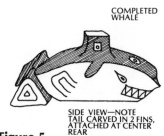

COMPLETED WHALE

SIDE VIEW—NOTE TAIL CARVED IN 2 FINS, ATTACHED AT CENTER REAR

Figure 5

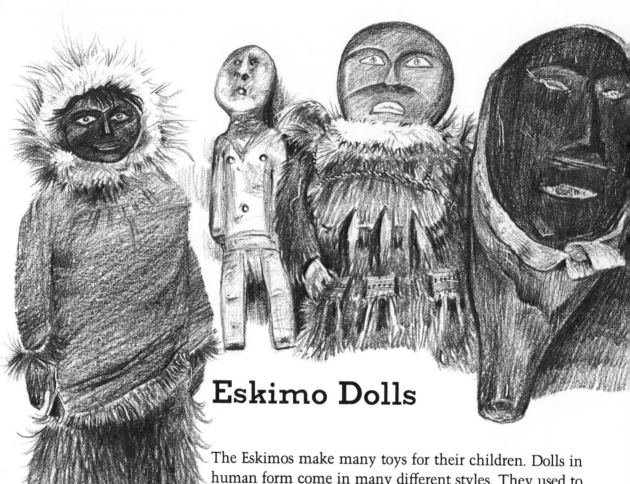

Eskimo Dolls

The Eskimos make many toys for their children. Dolls in human form come in many different styles. They used to be carved from wood or ivory or bone, and had features that were painted on, engraved, or carved in three dimensions. Sometimes just a carved head and neck were sewn to a body and clothing made of hide or cloth. Dolls resemble human beings in all ways. They look like little adults, with black hair and fur-trimmed hide clothes. Sometimes the dolls wear leggings and moccasins as well as an Eskimo parka with a fur-trimmed hood. Mother dolls sometimes carry tiny infant dolls inside their fur-lined hoods, just as real Eskimo mothers do.

Our doll model stands 8 inches (20.5 cm) tall. The clothes are made to fit this size. You can make the doll, or use a premade one, but fit the clothes to suit your doll, following the basic shapes. Make a man or a woman. Both men and women wear some kind of parka, boots, pants, and mittens. The woman's parka has a space in the back to hold a baby. Women may also wear cotton dresses over their parkas.

Materials you will need:
Wood or self-hardening clay or papier-mâché, whittling knife, soft deerskin, modeling tools, felt or cloth, scraps of fur (such as rabbit fur) for trim, needle and thread, glue, paint, black wool (or paint, for hair), colored felt-tip pens, scissors, tape measure, pins, chalk, black tape

The doll:
1. Carve or model the body from any material you wish. The body is a single piece. (See Figure 1.)

2. Mold the hands separately as shown. Make long pinched wrists with two needle holes poked through the upper part so that they can be sewn to the sleeves.

3. Make the head and face broad and flat. The features will be painted on later.

4. Let the basic forms dry.

The clothing:
1. To make the parka, follow the basic pattern. Adjust the measurements to fit the size of your doll.

2. Cut the deerskin, felt, or cloth 8 inches (20.5 cm) by 8 inches (20.5 cm).

3. Fold the cloth in half to 4 inches (10 cm) by 8 inches (20.5 cm), as shown in Figure 2.

4. Use chalk to mark the measurements and lines as shown. Note that the basic pattern is "T" shaped. The skirt can be slightly flared out as shown or the sides can be straight. Different tribes use different styles.

5. Cut along the lines as shown.

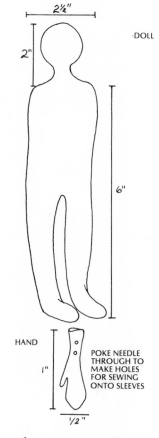

Figure 1

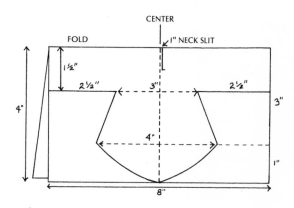

Figure 2

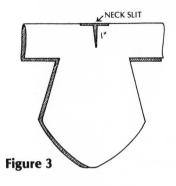

Figure 3

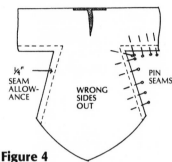

Figure 4

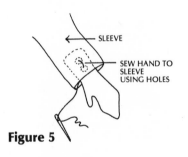

Figure 5

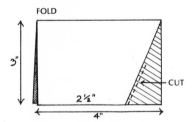

Figure 6

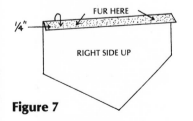

Figure 7

6. After cutting out the pattern, make a 1-inch (2.5-cm) center neck slit on the front panel (Figure 3).

7. Fold the cloth wrong sides out. Pin and sew the side seams, about ¼ inch (.5 cm) in from the edges (Figure 4).

8. Remove the pins and turn the piece right side out.

9. Sew or glue fur strips along the bottom hem, in front and in back. You can paint decorative patterns on the skirt if you wish. The Eskimos often embroider their designs.

10. Stick one hand up each sleeve and sew the cuff fabric to the wrist. Pass a needle through the hole in the wrist so that the thread that passes through the hand secures it well to the fabric. Brush a bit of glue onto the wrist and pinch fabric onto glued wrist to hold it well (Figure 5).

11. To make the parka hood, cut cloth 6 inches (15 cm) by 4 inches (10 cm). Fold cloth to 3 inches (7.5 cm) by 4 inches (10 cm).

12. Draw a diagonal line as shown, making the bottom edge 2 ½ inches (6.5 cm) (Figure 6). Cut along the diagonal line.

13. Spread out the piece as shown (Figure 7) with the right side up.

14. Fold over about ¼ inch (5 cm) of the long edge and sew or glue a fur strip to it for an edging.

15. Fold the piece as shown (Figure 8) with the wrong sides out.

16. Pin and sew a seam ¼ inch (.5 cm) deep in the diagonal edge, making the point of the hood. Remove the pins and turn right side out.

17. Pin the center seam line of the hood to the center back of the parka's neck hole (Figure 9).

18. Pin around the neck, joining the hood at the edge of the neck as far as it will go on each side of the center.

19. Sew a ¼-inch (.5-cm) seam along the edge. Remove the pins.

20. Paint features on the doll's head.

21. Glue black wool on the head for hair—either flat, or in braids (Figure 10).

22. Glue strips of fur around the doll's legs for leggings (Figure 11) and around the feet for boots. The soles of the boots can be a piece of black electrical tape, pressed onto the fur. Glue strips of fur around the sleeve cuffs, covering the wrist attachment.

23. Put the parka on the doll, carefully easing the neck opening over the head so that the hair is not disturbed.

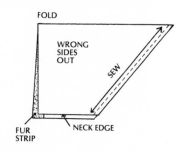

Figure 8

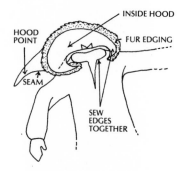

Figure 9

Figure 10

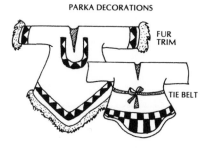

Figure 12

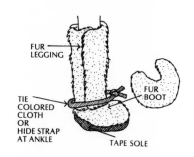

Figure 11

Index